How Are You "Being"?

How Are You "Being"?

Clergy Wellness in a Time of Uncertainty

Frederick J. Streets

PICKWICK *Publications* · Eugene, Oregon

HOW ARE YOU "BEING"?
Clergy Wellness in a Time of Uncertainty

Pickwick Publications
An Imprint of Wipf and Stock Publishers
199 W. 8th Ave., Suite 3
Eugene, OR 97401

www.wipfandstock.com

PAPERBACK ISBN: 978-1-6667-7809-0
HARDCOVER ISBN: 978-1-6667-7810-6
EBOOK ISBN: 978-1-6667-7811-3

Cataloguing-in-Publication data:

Names: Streets, Frederick J., author.

Title: How are you being : clergy wellness in a time of uncertainty / Frederick J. Streets.

Description: Eugene, OR : Pickwick Publications, 2024 | Includes bibliographical references.

Identifiers: ISBN 978-1-6667-7809-0 (paperback) | ISBN 978-1-6667-7810-6 (hardcover) | ISBN 978-1-6667-7811-3 (ebook)

Subjects: LCSH: Clergy—Psychology. | Clergy—Health and hygiene. | Pastoral care.

Classification: BV4398 .S86 2024 (paperback) | BV4398 .S86 (ebook)

VERSION NUMBER 07/05/24

To all clergy members

The work that clergy do is hard. It is good work. It is work that matters. And it matters that clergy take care of themselves.

Let us not become weary in doing good, for at the proper time we will reap a harvest if we do not give up. (Gal 6:9)

Contents

Acknowledgments

EXPRESSING MY GRATITUDE TO the Louisville Institute for providing me with the Pastoral Study Project grant does not adequately
articulate my appreciation for the time to rest, reflect, and carry
out research that this opportunity afforded me. I want to thank my
family for their love, support, and encouragement always, including during this time away from normal pastoral duties.

I turned to my friend and colleague Richard F. Mollica, MD,
founder and director of the Harvard Program in Refugee Trauma,
for advice on a research tool for this study project. He recom-
mended the Physician Well-Being Index of the Mayo Clinic. I
thank the Mayo Clinic for permission to apply this measurement
to the clergy under study.

Dr. Catherine Cook-Cottone gave permission for me to use
her Mindful Self-Care Scale (MSCS), which is a central part of this
study.

Mr. Nicholas Appleby, Yale Printing & Publishing Services,
and Mr. Aidan Appleby, a computer analysis consultant, provided
invaluable assistance in guiding this project. Nicholas Appleby de-
signed the website for this project.[1]

Dr. Jason Hotchkiss, a colleague of Dr. Cook-Cottone, researcher, and statistician, helped bring results of this project to

---

1. https://jerrystreets.org/clergy-well-being-surveys/.

life and aided in its completion. Dr. Hotchkiss is also an ordained minister and serves churches in the San Francisco Bay Area.

My gratitude extends to many colleagues at Yale Divinity School for their support of this project: Drs. Sarah Drummond, founding dean, Andover Newton at Yale; William Goettler, associate dean of Ministerial and Social Leadership, lecturer in parish leadership and church administration; Donyelle McCray, professor of homiletics; Andrew McGowan, dean and president of Berkeley Divinity School and McFaddin Professor of Anglican Studies and Pastoral Theology; Vernice Randall, associate dean of Admissions and Financial Aid, lecturer in homiletics; Maria LaSala, lecturer in history and polity of the Presbyterian Church and homiletics and director of the Reformed Studies Certificate Program. I also thank Tracy Johnson Russell, lecturer in divinity and coordinator at the Howard Thurman Center for Justice and Transformational Ministry at Hartford International University; and Benjamin Watts, director of the Black Minister's Certificate Program, Hartford International University.

This study would not have been possible without the support and wise counsel of Michael Ciba, area conference minister, Southwest Region, Southern New England Conference of the United Church of Christ; Terry Yasuko Ogawa, area conference minister, Northwest Region, Southern New England Conference of the United Church of Christ; Harry L. Riggs, executive minister, American Baptist Churches of Connecticut; and Keith King, senior pastor of the Christian Tabernacle Baptist Church in Hamden, Connecticut. Through their respective offices, these colleagues sent emails and reminders to clergy inviting them to participate in this study and announced this project in newsletters and other communication organs of their denominations. I also wish to thank to Yale Divinity School students Ms. Daisy Jones and Ms. Claire Weihe for taking notes at the focus group discussions.

Like a sculptor uses their skill to turn a stone into a work of beauty and art, I am deeply grateful for the assistance and guidance of Rona Johnston, editor extraordinaire.

A special note of appreciation is owed to the Dixwell Avenue Congregational United Church of Christ in New Haven, Connecticut, where I serve as senior pastor. Founded in 1820, Dixwell Church is the oldest African American Congregational church in the United States. The church supported my time away on sabbatical leave.

My deep appreciation to the entire staff of Wipf and Stock and Pickwick Publications for their contribution in bringing this project to life.

My deepest gratitude to my wife Annette; our children Bennett, Carolyn, and Tina; and daughter-in-love, Andrea, all of whose love and support make living life joyous.

And finally, I wish to express my deep gratitude to all the clergy who voluntarily participated in this study. At a time when overwork and additional demands were in many cases affecting their well-being, they were still willing to commit time and effort to sharing their personal experiences. This study would literally have been impossible without their contribution.

Reading Guide

I HOPE THIS BOOK will be a resource for anyone interested in self-care across the helping professions, especially in relation to how a sense of well-being is nurtured. While the study itself focuses on ministerial practices like parish ministry and also hospital or other institutional chaplaincies, the issues of stress and burnout faced by clergy in these fields are similar to challenges encountered by social workers, physicians, nurses, and other helping professionals. At their core, all are providing for the care of other human beings.

We cannot just think our way into better emotional, spiritual, and physical health. We require self-awareness, which comes with the capacity to be in touch with our feelings and then address the needs in us that those feelings signal. The findings of this study, which is focused on a defined set of mindfulness and self-care practices among specific clergy, demonstrate how crisis can open us to new ways of understanding ourselves and of how we might choose to be present in this world. I believe this dual aspiration is a universal human quest.

We live in a profoundly fatiguing age. From time to time, we need to pause and rest. But we also need to access our capacity to generate hope by what we do and how we show up in the world. My desire is that those reading this volume will be reminded of this ability, and even inspired, by clergy who found adaptability, resilience, and new meaning at a time of great instability.

Part One

Introduction

A Pastor's Perspective

I BREATHED DEEPLY AND felt a great relief when, in December 2021, I received notice from the Louisville Institute that I had been granted a sabbatical grant for pastors. I had been assisting my congregation nonstop for nearly three years as we all sought ways to cope with the COVID-19 pandemic. The shift to online worship services had required me to record at home, which meant quickly learning to use technology, including sound, lighting, and green-screen equipment. We held weekly Zoom congregational wellness and staff meetings. Our monthly church board and committee meetings were held either via Zoom or by means of telephone conference calls. I sent the congregation a monthly pastoral letter and communion kits. I visited those who were ill and offered pastoral guidance to others. There were funerals to organize and conduct, both for victims of COVID-19 and for those who had died of other causes. Some were held with only limited numbers at the graveside or as a small gathering at the church or a funeral home. All were available via Zoom to family members and friends not able to attend the service in person. My congregation, like all the world, were experiencing fear, vulnerability, and profound grief, results of all kinds of losses. And I continued to teach in line with Yale University COVID-19 protocols, reaching my students and conducting classes by Zoom. I got my first shots and then my booster. I also got diagnosed with COVID-19, but recovered quickly with the help of the medications that had not been available two years earlier.

I consider myself a self-aware person, and I practice various forms of self-care. However, in the moment I learned that I had the opportunity to take sabbatical, I was gripped with an awareness of how tired I had become from taking care of my family, from carrying out my pastoral duties, from supporting my students, and from looking after myself ever since the beginning of the pandemic.

I attended a meeting of faith leaders to reflect on the topic "Spiritual Self-Care in the Midst of Today's Challenges." The gathering was sponsored by the Meister Eckhart Center for Catholic and Dominican Life at Albertus Magnus College in Hamden, Connecticut. Our group consisted of Catholic, Protestant, and Jewish clergy and lay members. Sister Anne Kilbride, OP, led us in a guided opening meditation followed by two presentations given by two ministers, the Reverend Bonita Grubbs (Baptist) and the Reverend Lindasusan Ulrich (Universalist Unitarian).

Sister Kilbride framed her meditation by suggesting that we think of Jesus as a minister who gave and received compassion. The images she conjured were of Jesus having his feet washed by Mary and his asking for and receiving water at Jacob's well. She asked us to reflect on how we give and receive compassion from others. She noted times when the New Testament recorded Jesus as being "pressed on every side" and asked us what we do when we feel pressed.

We then each took a twig and observed it. The twig, broken off from its larger plant, had been separated from its origins, where it had received food and sunlight. Sister Kilbride had us imagine how in the twig's original home smaller insects had used it as a bridge or path and how birds had rested upon it. She encouraged us to consider what it is like when we feel separated, or broken off, from our ministries and their sources of nourishment and have the impression we can no longer serve as a bridge or pathway for others.

Ultimately, self-care is about letting go, about accepting our humanness. Then we can make room for others to journey. How we live and lead as clergy depends on our understanding of ourselves as ministers and of the world in which we are living at that moment. And understanding our human selves correlates with our self-care.

Ministry is being practiced today under uncertain social and global conditions, defined by the pandemic, political polarization, social unrest, and climate change. Many clergy and congregants experience a profound sense of anxiety about our world's future as they discern their life's direction. This is the context where ministry is done and where the church and its members search for their identity and a sense of belonging. Self-care is therefore imperative for the well-being of church leaders, church members, and society beyond.

Distress in a Global Pandemic

In the abstract for an article on chaplain burnout published in 2018, Jason Hotchkiss and Ruth Lesher recorded,

> The strongest protective factors against Burnout in order of strength were self-compassion and purpose, supportive structure, mindful self-awareness, mindful relaxation, supportive relationships, and physical care. For secondary traumatic stress, supportive structure, mindful self-awareness, and self-compassion and purpose were the strongest protective factors. Chaplains who engaged in multiple and frequent self-care strategies experienced higher professional quality of life and low Burnout risk.[1]

Religious organizations were recognizing that the pursuit of wellness among their clergy is a win for both clergy and members. In

---

1. Jason T. Hotchkiss and Ruth Lesher, "Factors Predicting Burnout among Chaplains: Compassion Satisfaction, Organizational Factors, and the Mediators of Mindful Self-Care and Secondary Traumatic Stress," *Journal of Pastoral Care & Counseling* 72 (2018) 86–98 (https://doi.org/10.1177/1542305018780655), abstract.

the spiritual care professional's journey toward wellness, mindful self-care is imperative.

During the COVID-19 pandemic, however, clergy fulfilled their ministerial duties in the midst of the unprecedented distress of the pandemic. Great distress has been recognized as potentially leading to depression, burnout, substance abuse, and other forms of unhealthy self-soothing behaviors.[2] Left unattended, such reactions can lead to physical, emotional, and spiritual decline, which in turn can affect the ability to provide pastoral leadership in a specific context.

The core question for this study of clergy during a period of extraordinary distress was "How are you 'being'?" The study was carried out in spring 2022. I was curious to know about the clergy's own responses to this distress and how their actions and reactions reflected their sense of self. In asking what sustains clergy living in a trauma-impacted world, I recognized I would be highlighting crucial skills needed for the practice of ministry today.

Answers to my question should not only help pastors in the field engage in self-support, but they would also surely help congregations and denominations be supportive of their clergy and give seminaries and divinity schools food for thought too.

Defining Self-Care

Self-care can be defined as the daily process of being aware of and attending to one's basic physiological and emotional needs, including the shaping of one's daily routine, relationships, and environment. Self-care is associated with positive physical health, emotional well-being, and good mental health.

Mindful self-care adds the component of mindful awareness. It is foundational work required for physical and emotional thriving. The steady and intentional practice of mindful self-care is seen as protective, for it can prevent the onset of mental health symptoms and job burnout and can improve work productivity.

2. Bessel van der Kolk, *The Body Keeps the Score: Brain, Mind, and Body in the Healing of Trauma* (New York: Viking, 2014).

How Can Self-Care Happen?

Many helping professions provide their practitioners with guidelines for what constitutes ethical and professional service. Central to these standards and parameters is an emphasis upon attending to one's own emotional, physical, and spiritual needs and receiving supervision (for clergy, often in the form of spiritual direction) in order at a minimum to do no harm and at best to provide professional care that involves one's use of the whole self. To give such care requires being aware of the values one holds and their impact upon one's professional behavior.

Many clergy work alone or in a siloed environment. Support from peers and/or their denomination may be hard to access and, indeed, hard to ask for. Throughout my professional career as clergy and clinical social worker, I have been helped immensely by the suggestions of a self-care protocol. This tool can help one's stewardship of one's self and one's good care of others. A self-care protocol can serve as a road map that empowers the user to plot their own path, to plan their way stations, to consider their destination. It can be particularly helpful when clergy travel alone, but they can interact with others at the stops they plan and on the roads they travel. Its contents—and its very existence—can remind clergy that they are not alone in their work, worries, and contributions to the welfare of others.

Part Two

Process

Planning

A RESEARCH PROPOSAL WAS submitted to the Pastoral Study Project at the Louisville Institute for assessment of the risk to human participants; the risk was deemed minimal, and the study was approved. Established guidelines for survey research were followed,[1] including planning content carefully and grouping by subject, a process aided by adapting existing survey tools. The survey commenced with a statement on informed consent. Assurances of anonymity and confidentially were to be provided in writing, and also contact information for the principal researcher.

Methodology

This exploratory study measured clergy well-being based upon responses to two survey instruments: one discerning wellness and the other concerning clergy self-care practices. It also collected demographic information about the respondents. Data was gathered first by these two surveys and subsequently through focus group

1. Kate Kelley et al., "Good Practice in the Conduct and Reporting of Survey Research," *International Journal for Quality in Health Care* 15 (2003) 261–66. https://doi.org/10.1093/intqhc/mzg031.

discussions, which involved a smaller voluntary sample of those who had completed the surveys. The voluntary participants in this study were randomly selected for these focus groups, where they reflected on the study results and shared their experiences with self-care practices. This added a qualitative element to how the clergy in this study describe their sense of well-being.

Survey Data Collection

A total of 650 clergy are listed as practicing within the Southern New England Conference of the United Church of Christ. American Baptist clergy in Connecticut number 103. Also identified were an additional 35 clergy representing the Episcopal Church in Connecticut, 9 Presbyterian, 3 Evangelical Lutheran Church of America, and 2 United Methodist.

A random sample of these clergy were invited via email to participant in a confidential online survey regarding their well-being and self-care practices. A total of 1,120 clergy were contacted.

The questionnaire was completed by participants in spring 2022.

Focus Group Data Collection

"Focus groups provide an opportunity to expand on data gathered previously by the researcher. . . . Interaction between participants can yield data not available through other data sources," note Donna Graham and John Bryan.[2] Initially 132 participants indicated an interest in being a part of a focus group to reflect on the study questions and results. These 132 respondents were randomly divided into groups of no more than ten members each and invited to attend a focus group meeting on Zoom. Some clergy had a change in their availability and were unable to attend. Eleven

2. Donna Graham and John Bryan, "How Many Focus Groups Are Enough: Focus Groups for Dissertation Research," Faculty Focus, Sept. 7, 2022, para. 6 (https://www.facultyfocus.com/articles/academic-leadership/how-many-focus-groups-are-enough-focus-groups-for-dissertation-research/).

focus groups sessions were held, with thirty-seven survey respondents participating in total. Twenty-seven focus group members identified as female, and ten as male. One identified as African American male, and one identified as African American female.

To quote Graham and Bryan again: "One focus group conducted well may be better than two or more that are less effective."[3] A focus group covenant and agenda or protocol were created to structure and guide the focus group discussions:

Covenant

- Each group participant is expected to hold in confidence all group content and discussion.
- Each group member will hold one another in care and contribute to the feeling of safety and support of one another in the group meeting.
- Zoom meetings will be recorded, unless any group member wishes that it not be recorded, for note-taking purposes.
- Names and other personal and/or professional identifying information of group participants will be held anonymously. Only denominational representations and main points of group discussions will be noted for reporting purposes.
- An administrative person, not a member of the group, will take group notes and adhere to the group covenant.

Agenda

1. Welcome, introductions, opening meditation
2. Sharing highlights of survey results
3. Reflections and discussion on questions like:

    - How do you relax?

---

3. Graham and Bryan, "How Many Focus Groups," para. 1.

- How do you check in with yourself regarding your well-being?
- Self-compassion: How do you show yourself the compassion and care you give to others?
- What areas are you now exploring to engage in self-care?

4. Other suggestions/comments

5. Closing meditation/prayer

Meditation and Prayer

The items below were read by the facilitator, followed by a moment of silence. Group members were then invited to comment on these selections.

> Jesus often withdrew to lonely places and prayed. (Luke 5:16)

> There is in every person an inward sea, and in that sea, there is an island, and, on that island, there is an altar and standing guard before that altar is the "angel with the flaming sword." Nothing can get by that angel to be placed upon that altar unless it has the mark of your inner authority. Nothing passes "the angel with the flaming sword" to be placed upon your altar unless it be a part of "the fluid area of your consent." This is your crucial link with the Eternal.[4]

> True courage comes when we decide to take a risk without knowing the outcome. It means being[,] showing up[,] and letting yourself be seen, despite the risk. When you show up in this way, you open yourself up [to] joy and connection, but you can only do it by accepting that there could be pain.[5]

---

4. Howard Thurman, *Meditations of the Heart* (Boston: Beacon, 1953), 15.

5. Brené Brown, as quoted in "There Is No Courage without Vulnerability," Intraconnections Counseling, Nov. 12, 2019 (Intraconnectionscounseling.com/ blog-1(2019)/there is-no-courage without vulnerability).

At the end of the group session, participants were invited to offer a blessing to the group.

Note-Taking

The sessions were recorded with the permission of the group. My assistant was introduced to the group and assigned to take notes of the session, although not as a visible on-screen member during the group session. The notes from the discussions were subsequently read with an eye to themes and suggestions, which together contextualized and added nuance to the survey results.

Tools of Analysis

Physician Well-Being Index (PWBI)

The Physician Well-Being Index (PWBI) was selected to operationalize overall well-being among spiritual care providers.

Originally created at the Mayo Clinic to assess the well-being of medical students, the PWBI uses just nine questions to assess six areas of distress—burnout, depression, stress, fatigue, and mental and physical quality of life.[6] It operates as an online self-assessment tool. It can enable immediate support for the participant, for the anonymous data it generates can be used to craft focused assistance. Its website notes that the PWBI has been variously validated and is now used by six hundred medical institutions and organizations worldwide, with applications not just for students but also for healthcare professionals, including physicians, nurses, and pharmacists.[7]

---

6. Liselotte N. Dyrbye et al., "Efficacy of a Brief Screening Tool to Identify Medical Students in Distress," *Academic Medicine* 86 (2011) 907–14 (https://doi.org/10.1097/ACM.0b013e31821da615).

7. https://www.mywellbeingindex.org.

Mindful Self-Care Scale (MSCS)

According to the website of developer Catherine Cook-Cottone, the Mindful Self-Care Scale (MSCS) is "intended to help individuals identify areas of strength and weakness in self-care behavior, as well as interventions that serve to improve self-care."[8] For this project, I employed with permission the MSCS-Standard, a thirty-three-item scale that measures the self-reported frequency of mindful self-care behaviors. The scale addresses six domains of self-care: "physical care, supportive relationships, mindful awareness, self-compassion and purpose, mindful relaxation, and supportive structure."[9]

Study Limitations

While the high response rate increases the validity of the results, we must not ignore the study's limitations. I could not, for example, account for variables such as congregational, denominational, and family demands. Personal factors and organizational structures could have influenced responses; indeed, societal pressure surely also plays a role here. Despite the promise of anonymity, clergy who were not practicing effective self-care might have been reluctant to take the survey, and in particular to attend the focus groups—or they might have been especially eager to participate.

In particular, this study does not address gendered or cultural forms of clergy awareness and self-care practice. Nor does it highlight the impact of greater experience in a specific professional position. Both factors—(1) gender and cultural influences, and (2) experience—should certainly be mined in further research.

8. https://www.catherinecookcottone.com/research-and-teaching/mindful-self-care-scale/.

9. Catherine P. Cook-Cottone and Wendy M. Guyker, "The Development and Validation of the Mindful Self-Care Scale (MSCS): An Assessment of Practices That Support Positive Embodiment," *Mindfulness* 9 (2018) 161–75, abstract.

Part Three

Findings

THIS RESEARCH USED DESCRIPTIVE, analytical, and inferential methods to examine self-care practices and the well-being of spiritual care providers. The data collected has been assembled within pie charts or column charts for ease of communication and to encourage discussion. Tables 1 through 21 illustrate demographics and church context; tables 22 through 64 illustrate methods of self-care; tables 65 through 73 illustrate clergy well-being.

For the questions asked in the online survey, see appendix 1.

For the testing of the four research hypotheses by means of the data collected in the surveys, see appendix 2.

Who Participated?

Tables 1 through 3 display selected demographic information for the participants in the survey.

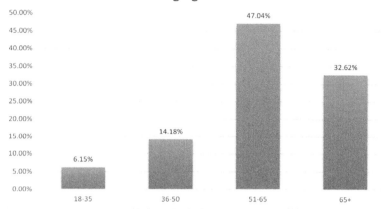

Age Ranges of Clergy Surveyed
Avg Age: 59.94

Table 1

Gender Self-Identification of Clergy Surveyed

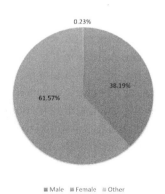

■ Male ■ Female ■ Other

Table 2

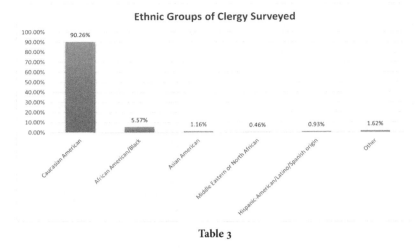

Table 3

Females were in the majority (65.0 percent). Age range was between twenty-five and eighty-seven years. Notably, almost 80 percent of respondents were aged fifty-one or over.

The mainline Protestant denominations are known to have a high percentage of Caucasian Americans (86.0 percent). Caucasian Americans (92.9 percent) formed the vast majority among respondents, followed by African Americans (4.3 percent), who were represented slightly more than the average across among the mainline denominations (3.0 percent)—African Americans' representation among study participants and mainline denominations was much less than among the general population (13.8 percent). A similar pattern existed for other ethnicities, where clergy participation was lower than their presence in the denominations in which they were serving and much lower than the general population.

Relationship with Institutional Church

Tables 4 to 7 illustrate respondents' reported experience as working clergy.

14

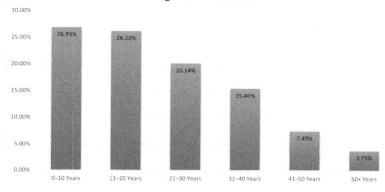

Table 4

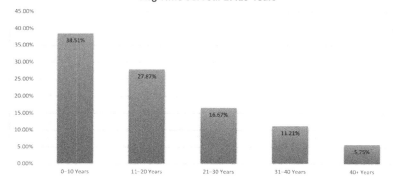

Table 5

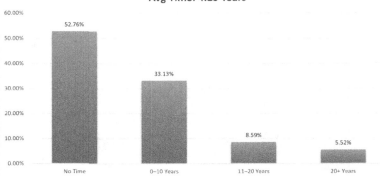

Institutional/Chaplain Time Served
Avg Time: 4.29 Years

Table 6

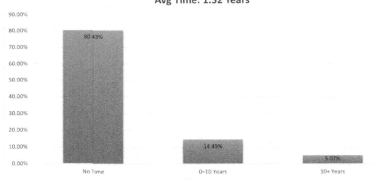

Denominational Officer/Executive Leader Time Served
Avg Time: 1.52 Years

Table 7

Although demographically the respondents were much more likely to be aged fifty-one or above, almost half had been serving as professional clergy for under twenty years. Just under half of the respondents had experience as clergy outside parish ministry, as clergy to institutions or as chaplains. While 80 percent of the respondents had no experience in higher leadership roles, 5 percent had served in such roles for over ten years.

Worship during the Pandemic

Tables 8 through 11 illustrate how worship was provided during the pandemic.

Table 8

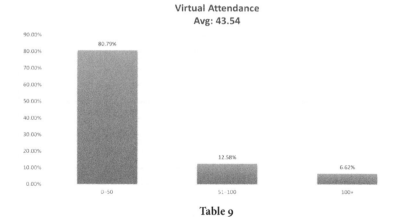

Table 9

In-Person Attendance
Avg: 56.59

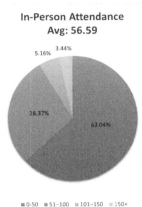

■ 0-50 ■ 51–100 ■ 101–150 ■ 150+

Table 12

Number of Months Church Was Online
Avg: 18.52 Months

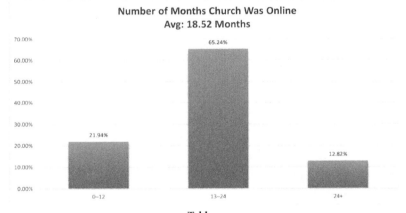

Table 11

Although the figures in these charts could suggest attendance fell when worship was online, we must be wary of such assumptions. More than one person may, for example, be watching on a single screen.

Staffing of Church

Tables 12 through 16 illustrate the professional community at each church.

Full-Time vs. Part-Time

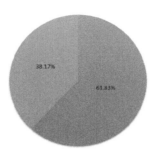

Table 12

Primary Care Responsibilities

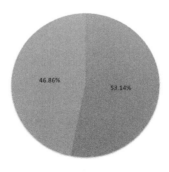

Table 13

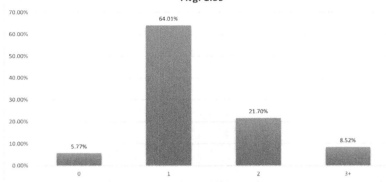

Table 14

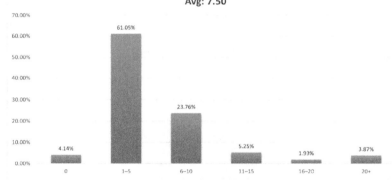

Table 15

Number of Tech Staff
Avg: 1.38

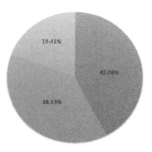

19.41%

42.06%

38.53%

■ 0   ■ 1-2   ■ 3+

Table 16

Almost two thirds of respondents were sole pastors. A majority worked with small staffs of one to five people, and 4 per cent had no additional staff. The number of technical staff was particularly relevant for experiences during COVID-19, and over 40 percent of respondents had no paid technical staff.

Impact of COVID-19

Tables 17 and 18 illustrate two particular stress points created by COVID-19.

Conflicts Concerning COVID Protocols

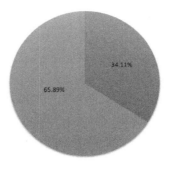

■ Yes ■ No

Table 17

Number of Tech Staff
Avg: 1.38

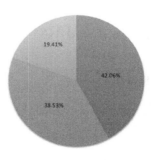

■ 0 ■ 1–2 ■ 3+

Table 18

Church leaders found themselves needing to recruit, become, or rely upon those with technical media skills to reach out to the congregation and community cloistered by COVID-19 (table 18).

Primary Care Responsibilities

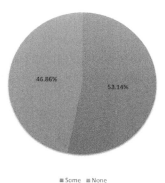

∎ Some ∎ None

Table 19

Some members of the clergy in the study indicated that they were the primary caretakers of relatives, and this responsibility added to the pressures and stress of their work as clergy (table 19).

Conflicts Concerning COVID Protocols

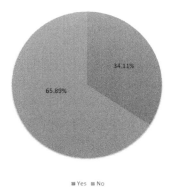

∎ Yes ∎ No

Table 20

Some clergy reported that deciding upon a COVID-19 protocol of care, such as whether to require masking and social distancing when on church property or gathering for worship or other meetings, was an important agenda item that needed to be discussed and resolved by the leadership of the church. Although the majority in the study (65.9 percent) indicated no conflict in addressing this issue, resolving the matter had to be done in a manner that garnered generous cooperation and consensus by the congregation (graph 20). Attending to this item required church leaders to use their conflict resolutions skills in an atmosphere of public health high anxiety.

Financial Impact of COVID Personally/Professionally

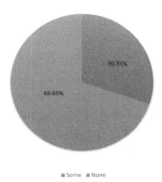

■ Some ■ None

Table 21

Conflict and financial concerns can have significant impact on mental well-being. One third of respondents reported conflict over COVID-19 protocols. A slightly smaller percentage reported direct personal or professional impact on their financial well-being.

We turn now to the responses to questions exploring self-care practices among the respondents during the restrictions of the COVID-19 pandemic.

Relaxation

Tables 22 through 27 illustrate the uptake of methods of relaxation, with results summarized in table 28.

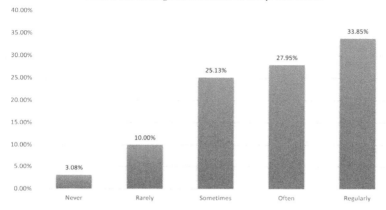

Table 22

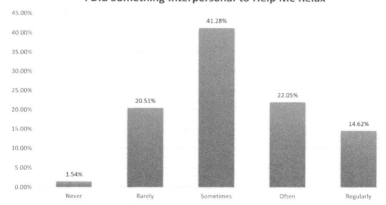

Table 23

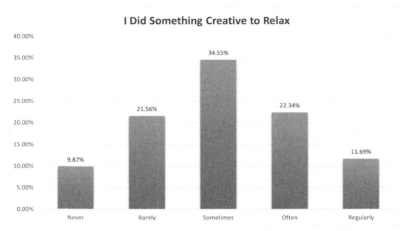

Table 24

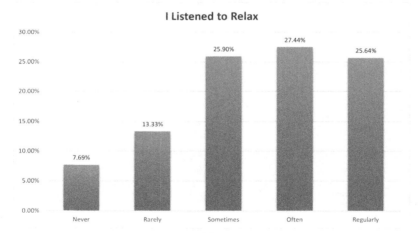

Table 25

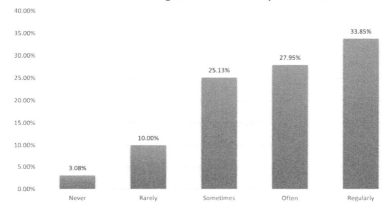

Table 22

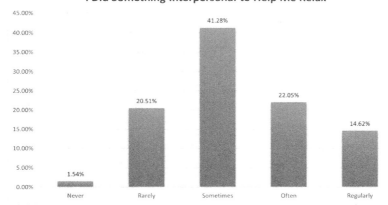

Table 23

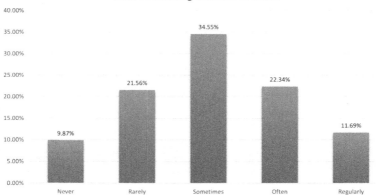

I Did Something Creative to Relax

Table 24

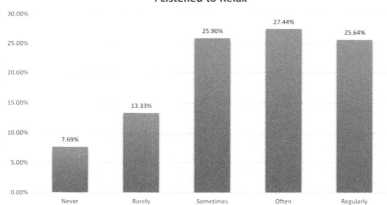

I Listened to Relax

Table 25

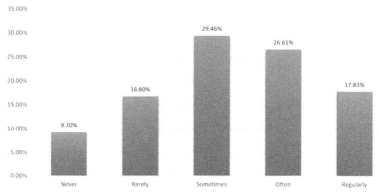

Table 26

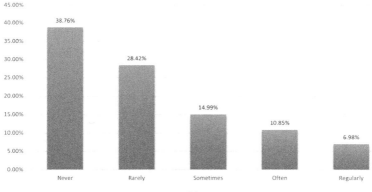

Table 27

The results in this section were combined to produce the following chart. The higher the individual's score, the more positive their overall replies to queries about undertaking mindful relaxation.

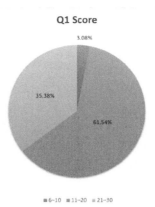

Table 28

Physical Care

Tables 29 through 36 illustrate how frequently participants cared in various ways for their physical health, with the results summarized in table 37.

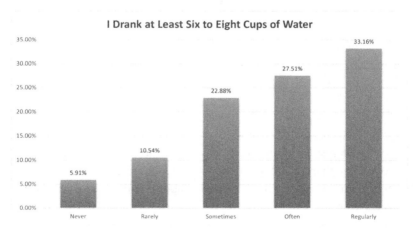

Table 29

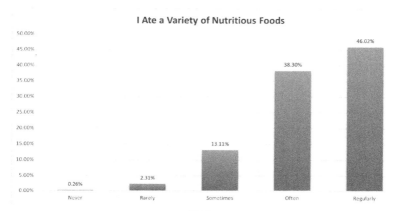

I Ate a Variety of Nutritious Foods

- Never: 0.26%
- Rarely: 2.31%
- Sometimes: 13.11%
- Often: 38.30%
- Regularly: 46.02%

Table 30

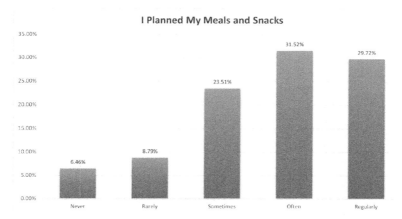

I Planned My Meals and Snacks

- Never: 6.46%
- Rarely: 8.79%
- Sometimes: 23.51%
- Often: 31.52%
- Regularly: 29.72%

Table 31

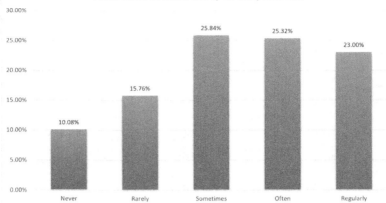

Table 32

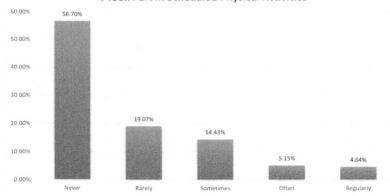

Table 33

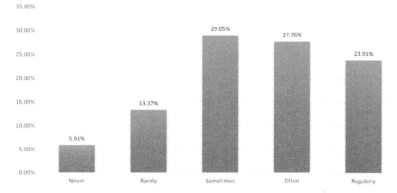

Table 34

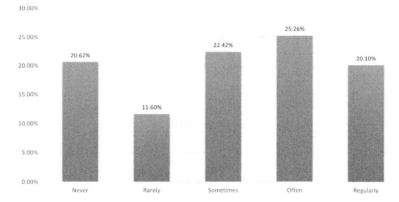

Table 35

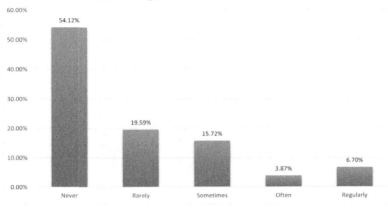

Table 36

The results in this section were combined to produce the following chart. The higher the individual's score, the more positive their replies to queries about undertaking physical care.

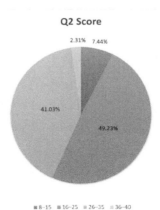

Table 37

Self-Compassion and Purpose

Tables 38 through 43 illustrate how frequently participants showed self-compassion and identified purpose in their lives, with the results summarized in table 44.

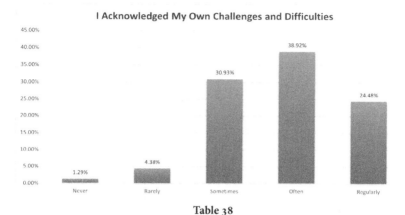

Table 38

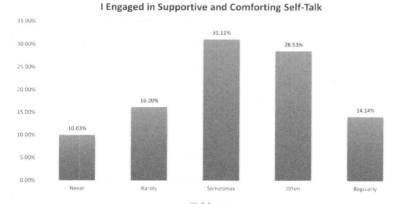

Table 39

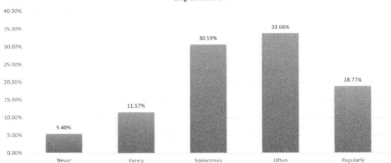

Table 40

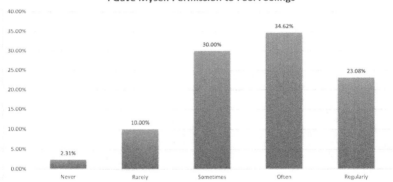

Table 41

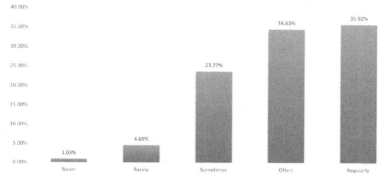

Table 42

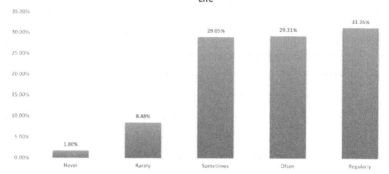

Table 43

The results in this section were combined to produce the following chart. The higher the individual's score, the more positive their replies to queries about undertaking self-compassion.

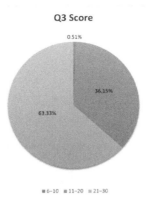

Q3 Score

0.51%

36.15%

63.33%

■ 6–10 ■ 11–20 ■ 21–30

Table 44

Supportive Relationships

Tables 45 through 49 illustrate how frequently participants accessed support from those around them, with the results summarized in table 50.

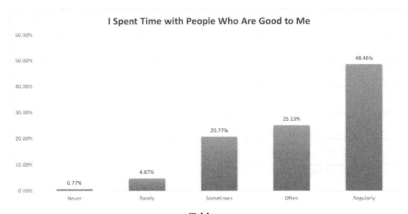

I Spent Time with People Who Are Good to Me

48.46%

25.13%

20.77%

4.87%

0.77%

Never   Rarely   Sometimes   Often   Regularly

Table 45

FINDINGS

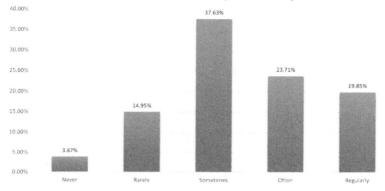

Table 46

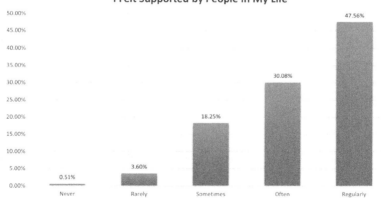

Table 47

I Felt Confident That People in My Life Would Respect My Choice if I Said No

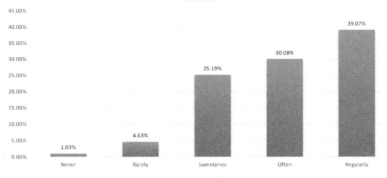

Table 48

I Felt That I Had Someone Who Would Listen to Me if I Became Upset

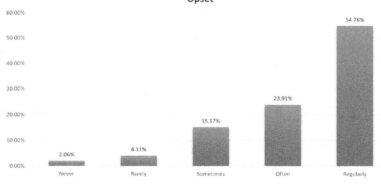

Table 49

The results in this section were combined to produce the following chart. The higher the individual's score, the more positive their replies to queries about access to supportive relationships.

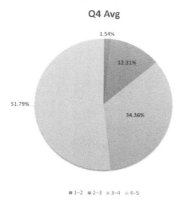

Table 50

Supportive Structure

Tables 51 through 54 illustrate how frequently their physical and temporal surroundings supported the participants, with the results summarized in table 55.

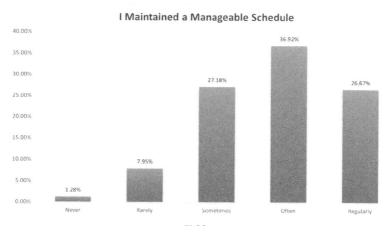

Table 51

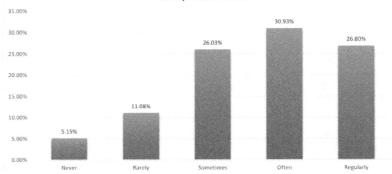

Table 52

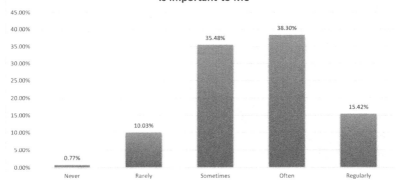

Table 53

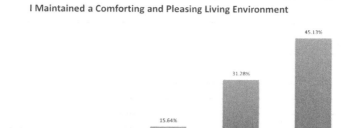

I Maintained a Comforting and Pleasing Living Environment

Table 54

The results in this section were combined to produce the following chart. The higher the individual's score, the more positive their replies to queries about access to supportive structures.

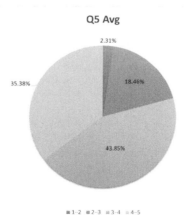

Q5 Avg

■ 1–2 ■ 2–3 ■ 3–4 ■ 4–5

Table 55

Mindful Awareness

Tables 56 through 59 illustrate how frequently participants experienced constructive personal awareness, with the results summarized in table 60.

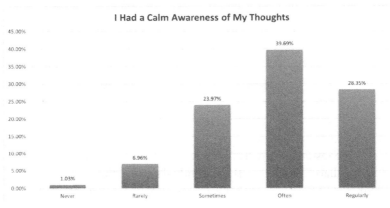

Table 56

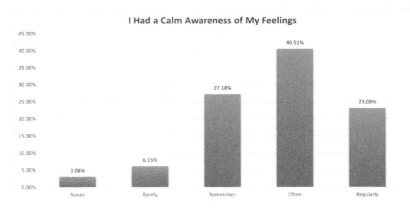

Table 57

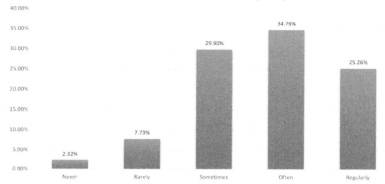

Table 58

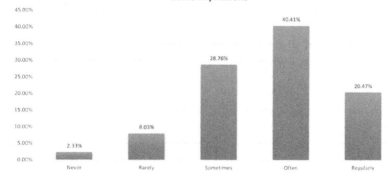

Table 59

The results in this section were combined to produce the following chart. The higher the individual's score, the more positive their replies to queries about practicing mindful awareness.

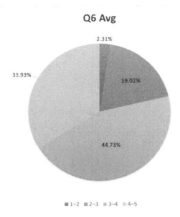

Table 60

Self-Care Overview

Tables 61 through 63 illustrate how frequently participants deliberately engaged with self-care, with the results summarized in table 64.

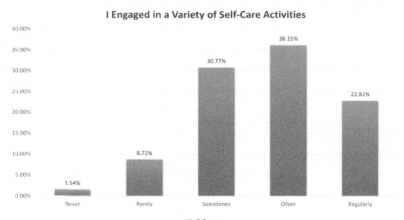

Table 61

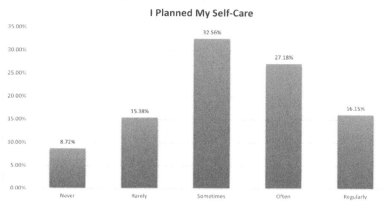

Table 62

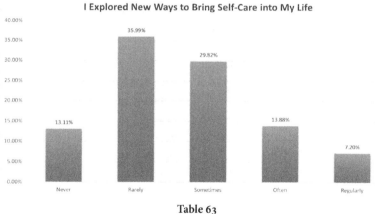

Table 63

The results in this section were combined to produce the following chart. The higher the individual's score, the more positive their replies to queries in the self-care overview.

Q7 Avg

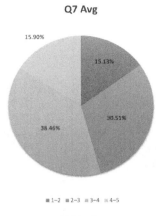

Table 64

And, finally, we turn to a third set of charts that illustrate responses to questions exploring well-being during the restrictions of the COVID-19 pandemic.

The Physician Well-Being Index, on which the following statements is based, is a negative measure of well-being, meaning this instrument takes a deficit perspective, measuring lack. For questions 1 through 7 (tables 65 through 71) respondents were responding to questions to which a positive answer (colored blue in each chart) indicates that they *are not* thriving. For the final two statements (tables 72 and 73), the reverse is the case—agreement with the statement suggests they *are* thriving.

In the Past Month, Have You Felt Burned Out from Work?

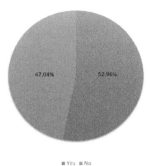

■ Yes ■ No

Table 65

In the Past Month, Have You Felt Hardened Emotionally from Work?

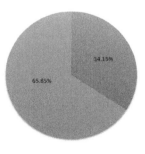

■ Yes ■ No

Table 66

In the Past Month, Have You Felt Down, Depressed, or Hopeless?

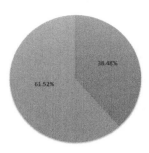

Table 67

In the Past Month, Have You Fallen Asleep While Sitting Inactive in a Public Place?

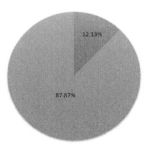

Table 68

In the Past Month, Have You Felt That Things Have Piled Up Such That You Cannot Overcome Them?

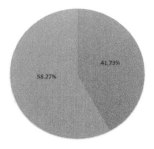

41.73%

58.27%

■ Yes ■ No

Table 69

During the Past Month, Have You Been Bothered by Emotional Problems?

40.81% 59.19%

■ Yes ■ No

Table 70

During the Past Month, Has Your Physical Health Interfered with Your Ability to Do Daily Work?

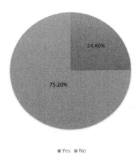

24.80%

75.20%

■ Yes ■ No

Table 71

My Work Schedule Leaves Me Enough Time for My Personal/Family Life

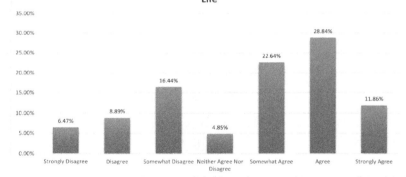

Table 72

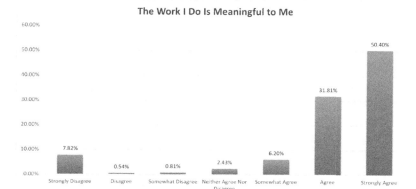

Table 73

Thematic Results from the Focus Groups

The focus group participants generally expected that the self-care study would highlight challenges for many of the respondents. That expectation stemmed from awareness of their own well-being and that of friends and colleagues. They were also sensitive to the media discussions of how COVID-19 propelled an episode of "quiet quitting."

Clergy who are positive about self-care and practice self-care themselves were thought more likely to have completed the survey. One participant noted that a friend had not participated because their wellness score would be "so bad."

A good number of participants spoke of self-care as a part of ministry, even a large part. But the balance had been intensified by the reality of COVID-19, in particular through compassion fatigue and vicarious suffering. The world was, in the words of one focus group participant, "depressing and heartbreaking and creative and challenging."

Faith: "It has been helpful to name that it has been hard"

Central theological beliefs were acknowledged as pillars in a time of crisis: one participant cited free will and agency as galvanizing when "things seemed simply too much."

Self-care was found by participants in interior spiritual practice, especially prayer. "I am blown away by how much God loves us," said one participant as they spoke of prayer as a source of calm and relaxation. Contemplative prayer in community on Zoom twice a day brought opportunity and routine. Meditative prayer was a source for several participants, one of whom noted how they used prayer while climbing and descending stairs to center themselves before and after seeing patients as part of their chaplaincy work.

Jesus was a model for one participant when it came to the demands of innovative forms of ministry: "Jesus was on the move," an inspiration for the participant's own ministry to similarly "explore and experiment."

Modeling by the pastor, too, was highlighted: "I do not want to teach or preach a word that I am not living."

One group noted that "self-care" is already part of the Christian life, beyond that "overused" terminology. They proposed taking up the language of "Sabbath" and "rest."

Yet, while faith was seen as sustaining, it needed to be accessed: one participant, for example, noted a greater willingness within their community of practice to take up bodily self-care than to address spiritual health and awareness of God in their life.

Pandemic Experiences: "I've never worked harder in my life"

Even as some participants spoke of the personal pressures of being a pastor during the pandemic, positive changes were also acknowledged.

At its core, ministry had to be performed differently, the participants agreed. What it was to act as a minister changed: unable to go house to house, they communicated via Zoom, Facebook Live, and sitting in driveways.

The challenges of learning to pastor online were evident. *Adaptability* was a key term here. One participant felt all their traditional skills were no longer useful—everything had to be re-learned. Another found online communication incredibly draining, so they kept worship very simple, with no live streaming. For another, the heightened demands on the pastor seemed to go unnoticed by their congregation. Another congregation was "anti-tech," even rejecting microphones during in-person worship as part of their search for intimacy; the novel need for online services and meetings was entirely counter to this church's ethos.

Yet at the same time another participant noted that since the online service needed to be prerecorded, it made them have the service prepared by the previous Thursday, releasing some pressure and allowing them to integrate the message into their own life before teaching it. One found that they work better at home, although they needed to find a way to communicate this to their congregations. Another shared that when working from home on Mondays, they are able to use time when baking for prayer and reflection.

And combining new media and needs during the pandemic, another participant made weekly three-minute videos about self-care for the congregation.

Community: "It is really only in community that we can find God in each other"

Again and again, participants raised the importance of community, whether in the form of friends and family, their congregation, or fellow pastors.

For one participant, a good home life was the most significant coping strategy. For another, it was a source of stability. Investment in family was deemed vital, including by one pastor whose earlier marriage had ended in divorce.

They also found that having friends outside their own church community was a fine opportunity. One participant talked of a relationship with three other couples—"we kept each other as healthy as possible and were honest with our feelings and behaviors." They could anchor each other through the years, when buffeted by life and ministry.

Fellow pastors were for many participants a source of support. Here was an opportunity, one participant noted, to explore the question "How are we growing and changing as faithful people?" These groups, they also observed, can be configured and reconfigured according to the needs of individual members. It was also noted that fellow pastors in the same geographical area who were not necessarily in the same denomination can also be a source of support.

The denomination can foster opportunities for pastors to be together in constructive ways. Official denomination meetings that "go on forever" are not the same as investment in clergy care that brings them together for fun and to decompress.

But the professional implications for such groups were also very real: "I never feel comfortable venting to other clergy, I might be shamed."

One participant was concerned and curious about the correlation between congregational health and clergy well-being. But the congregation was not necessarily the source of stress for the pastor. Pastors noted the support they felt from their congregation. In some instances the support was from individual members—for example, in encouraging the pastor to take time for themselves. In another instance it was congregational leadership that made the same recommendation.

Activity: "Sometimes you need to break out and do something crazy"

"I'm aware that my congregation understand me outside of being a pastor," one clergyperson noted. And indeed, participants repeatedly noted how their activities beyond the church fostered their well-being and thus their ability to serve in their spiritual capacity.

One participant highlighted the need to have multiple strategies, for any single strategy might not be available at a certain time. And changing a routine, another proposed, can be a way to tackle stress. Another participant had recognized that their self-care method depended on the type of stress they faced. When agitated, they try to walk; when tired, they might do a puzzle; when numbed, they seek to access their creativity—"I took up quilting during the pandemic, it's my therapy."

Physical activities and hobbies were seen as connection with God. As one new bird-watcher noted, "If we are awake and aware to God's world that is one way people can be centered." Several participants cited the importance of walking, sometimes in relation to prayer or engagement with the nature of God's world.

A remarkable range of other activities mentioned included gardening, golf, cooking, tennis, swimming, dancing, and yoga. It was noted that sometimes the need to do something other than work can become apparent because of exhaustion, but that exhaustion can also deplete motivation, especially for physical exercise.

For one participant, reading poetry with a spouse was "a holy moment." Music was a repeated theme, both music making and listening—bell ringing, piano playing, hymn singing. For another participant, "studying was also a great way to relax, with a few classes in biblical Greek and Hebrew."

Participants looked to books as resources: One participant learned the basics of relaxation from *The Relaxation Response*, by Herbert Benson, who forty years ago advocated for meditation as a means to reduce blood pressure.[1] Another turned to Howard Thurman's *Meditations of the Heart* for meditation and prayers. Others spoke of seeking to understand the responses around them through Bowen family systems theory or to gain insight through the Enneagram.

"I am very interested in the body," stated one participant. They continued, "Integrating daily and weekly self-care practices has been life-saving. Right now, it is walking." Caring for the body was an investment in the self and the congregation. "I have really struggled with severe migraine headaches," commented one participant, "and have committed to a monthly massage—which I wish didn't have a price tag, but I have a willingness to prioritize health." Another participant shared that once a week they visit a

1. Herbert Benson, *The Relaxation Response* (New York: Morrow, 1975).

reflexologist, who massages their feet for forty-five minutes—"It helps me with sermons," they noted.

A participant asked themself the question "If I were a parishioner, what would I offer them?" Often their exploration of that question resulted in greater self-awareness, a central theme of many discussions. Journaling was seen as a key self-care strategy, sometimes tied to a particular time of day. Also noteworthy, one participant proposed, is the idea of "holding space." In community, "holding space" allows one person to share with the others present, who sit with the sharer, without jumping in with questions and advice. In the same way, the individual can hold space for themselves, in a practice of self-acknowledgment that leads to self-awareness.

Denominational Support: "Who is the pastor's pastor?"

Denominational support was front and center in the discussions. Greater support would bring great benefits to both pastor and congregation. One participant recorded that their congregation did not understand the need for self-care, and therefore any contribution by the denomination would be very useful. As one ABC clergyperson asked, "Who is the pastor's pastor?"

The practicalities of denomination support were recognized. Even as one participant shared that they think that the denomination is providing abundant resources for pastor support, another acknowledged that denominational capacity has its limits.

The suggestions offered by participants were often concrete:

- Create the opportunity for a sole pastor to have one Sunday "off" each month, with cover provided by the same person, to create stability for the congregation

- Incentivize congregations to grant their pastors a sabbatical or vacation, and to respect their Sabbath

- Have congregations compose job descriptions that ensure time off for rest, vacation, study, etc.

- In each homiletics courses, teach preaching to a camera—
  that prior experience would have greatly lessened the shock
  during COVID-19

One specific form of denomination interaction that was repeatedly raised concerned the benefits of having a spiritual director. "During the pandemic I almost doubled the amount of time I
spent with my spiritual director; her wisdom was very useful."

Often the denominational focus turned to the training that
the pastors had received. "The idea that you can go away and pray
and fix everything is not going to work in this day and age," noted
one participant. One focus group, for example, was in no doubt
that self-care should be taught in polity courses. An advocate of
meditation could not remember the subject being addressed in
preparation for pastoring. Openness to other fields of thought,
such as psychology or management, would be constructive, helping self-care strategies be multiple and dynamic.

Clinical pastoral education had helped the most for pastoral
ministry, was one comment, while another participant noted, "A
full-time internship program should be a requirement of divinity students." Self-assessment and family system tools would be a
helpful for seminarians and active clergy to learn about themselves
and have greater self-awareness.

Before Pastoring: "I had to take care of myself"

Several participants looked back to the time before they were pastors, even to childhood, to explore their own attitude to self-care.
Indeed, one participant shared that he did not grow up with good
examples of clergy self-care since both his parents were ministers
and they had devoted their time only to the congregation and not
to their own lives.

The family of origin in several instances had a key role, both
positively (encouraging self-care) and negatively (making self-care
necessary). Spiritual development at an early age had been a pillar
through childhood and then beyond, including into pastorhood:

one participant reflected on going to Sunday school and learning about Christ and taking those lessons to heart. Where for one participant spiritual seeking as a high schooler had meant learning about Zen Buddhism, for another it had involved attending a Bahá'í temple and learning to meditate.

Becoming More Mature: "The gap between knowing and doing has closed"

Several participants noted age and experience as vital to their resilience but also to their commitment to self-care. Looking back, one participant could see where they might have acted differently. Age had brought another participant a sense of calm and a groundedness that enabled a more relaxed approach to life's challenges, including interpersonal ones.

Another participant reflected on a bad burnout experience early on in their career, so much so that they needed to leave ministry, and then come back; that experience had left them, they felt, more prepared for the demands of being a pastor during the pandemic.

Boundaries: "Openness with the congregation does leave you vulnerable, but Jesus was vulnerable"

Boundaries could be a fraught topic in the focus groups. For a good number of participants, boundaries were essential to pastor health. It was observed that "what feeds us is helping others and the community, but this can also be depleting for personal and family life." One participant noted that they believed their role to be to build the community among the faith community without them themselves being pulled in past their boundaries as a pastor. The pastor's boundaries might, however, not be respected, especially, one participant noted, with so many ways to communicate with the pastor now in place. Physical distance from the community was deemed by a supply preacher to be a benefit, a point echoed by an interim pastor.

One participant shared that an unhealthy congregation made them better at boundaries and self-care, whereas a healthy church has made them drop their boundaries and want to participate more.

But when advocating for close attachment to the community, another participant did voice a contrary position: "We need to be our community's lead disciples."

Waiting Too Long: "If I was burned out, how could I have the bandwidth for an application for a sabbatical?"

One story shared during a focus group was presented by a participant who postponed their planned sabbatical but then subsequently "hit the wall." Fortunately, their church offered a sabbatical. As part of that time of rest, healing, and exploration, the participant attended a retreat at Assisi, Italy. "There were moments of deep grief and deep joy . . . I needed to be present with myself . . . with a simple prayer, 'You are here and I am here.'" They returned with the mantra "respond, not react."

This story was echoed by a participant who spoke of a mentality that means that unless someone is in trouble, they will not work to develop self-care strategies. Struggle and pain seemed to them to be the cue to act: "I don't know how to get Homo sapiens to do anything unless there is pain involved." In a less dramatic but all-too-realistic statement, another participant noted that taking time away can be a source of feelings of guilt for a pastor.

Another participant shared generational words of wisdom: "My father was a pastor, and he told me, there will always be more work for you to do . . . when it comes time for your vacation, take it; if the work is urgent, someone will do it while you are gone."

After the Pandemic: "Things are changing so much"

One participant shared that they feel they have some form of post-COVID 19 (or post-lockdown) PTSD following all the stresses, accompanied by a lack of sleep. That diagnosis, they recognized, is not clinically correct, but undoubtedly the experience had significant impact on their health.

Pastors, it was proposed, must become better advocates for themselves towards church leadership. In other professions, such advocacy would exist without question.

The rupture caused one pastor to rethink their identity: "There are a lot of churches that are not going to make it. Who are we if we aren't who we always were? How do you pastor to smaller congregations? Will this be a St. Paul environment rather than Constantine? I would have a hard time going back into ministry during this time."

Change, it was recognized, is not easy: "I agree the whole nature of being church needs to evolve to something new . . . but the people who are in the pews are having to cling to what they have always known."

Another participant stressed the need to find joy again—in being clergy and in serving the faithful.

One participant is exploring with their spiritual director "what it means to have a God-centered relationship . . . how can I live the faith that I am attempting to model with my congregation." Their recommendation was for clergy to go on retreat weeks, especially silent retreats. Life coaching, they stressed, is not the same as spiritual direction. This spiritual dimension was also found in the words of a participant who spoke of how writing and transcribing prayers was a practice developed during the pandemic, helping them understand monastic scribes. Here was a spiritual journey when no one could travel.

Hope was also present in these focus groups: "In ten years I want to be where God wants me to be; I see no reason to stop doing this. I am grateful to have been called into ministry, where I can give my most energetic years."

And with the pandemic came a new self-understanding: "I am thinking about retiring in the next six years. Recently I was scared with what to do with the days when I retire . . . part of my spiritual practice now is imagining what I would do with the day if I did not go to the church."

Participation in this study: "Your survey has me thinking about who I am, and rethinking my call to ministry, and we all know who that call is from"

Many of the participants expressed gratitude for the opportunity to participate in the study ("I feel enriched and encouraged to continue this work") and to share self-care and mindfulness resources. Some were interested in continuing to learn more about one another and their work.

The survey was inherently revealing. One participant shared: "I was struck by the questions that prompted me to realize 'oh this is a problem.' I was able to have conversations with people and colleagues about these questions. The process of answering these questions was a sign of recovering some balance."

A participant expressed the hope that this study would be used by their denomination, not just "filed away." Perhaps, for example, covenants between pastor and congregation will be more explicit about self-care, including vacation, study time, and sabbaticals.

Lessons from the Focus Groups

What does it profit us if in gaining the world we lose our souls?
(Matt 16:26; Luke 9:25)

This caution is relevant for religious leaders as they think about their goals for their sacred work in the church. It can be difficult for clergy to separate their sense of self from the activities they perform, as is frequently evident when clergy retire. Yet clergy-people are more than the actions their roles require.

The impact of the pandemic impressed upon many of the clergy in this study a need to maintain a holistic perspective on who they are and what they do, in and beyond having a formal ministerial role. Self-care and mindfulness practices while doing ministry can help clergy balance their role expectations and their broader perception of themselves. The goal is to be aware of, or perhaps recover, one's authentic self.

Thirty years before COVID-19, when speaking of spirituality and leadership, Parker Palmer noted,

> A leader is a person who has an unusual degree of power to project on other people his or her shadow, or his or her light. A leader is a person who has an unusual degree of power to create the conditions under which other people must live and move and have their being—conditions that can either be as illuminating as heaven or as shadowy as hell. A leader is a person who must take special responsibility for what's going on inside him or herself, inside his or her consciousness, lest the act of leadership create more harm than good.[2]

And Parker cited Vaclav Havel: "Consciousness precedes being, and not the other way around."

With leadership comes responsibility, Palmer proposed, and a vital element of that responsibility is self-awareness. More recently, many clergy were compelled by the COVID-19 pandemic and social and political unrest to engage in deep reflection, thinking and listening to their own souls in an effort to cope with the stress and to seek guidance though the crisis. This process allowed for further discernment of who they were and how they wanted to be and live as human beings and pastoral leaders. It also acquainted some members of the clergy with a deeper understanding of their vulnerability and "shadow" side. Even as a new sense of self and self-agency, or consciousness, is emerging among some clergy, other clergy recognize a deep personal insecurity. Questions about their identity and self-worth have been exacerbated

2. Parker J. Palmer, *Insights on Leadership Service, Stewardship, Spirit, and Servant-Leadership*, edited by Larry C. Spears (New York: Wiley, 1990), 7.

by the combination of ongoing challenges within their ministries and the added burden of the acute phases of COVID-19 and the ongoing racial, social, and political conflicts of our time.

Commenting on insecurity among people in power, Parker recorded,

> If you're ever with people (or an organization led by a person) who know "all the way" down who they are, whose identity doesn't depend on a role which might be taken away at any moment, you are with people and in settings which give you identity, which empower you to be someone. I think that's a core issue in the spirituality of leadership—because the great spiritual gift that comes as one takes the inward journey is to know for certain that who I am does not depend on what I do. . . . Identity . . . depends only on the simple fact that I am a child of God, valued and treasured for what I am.[3]

While Palmer is thought provoking on spiritual leadership, the extraordinary challenges of the pandemic years, with their threat of global destruction and social unrest, brought a new reality that tempers the case he made. His "inward journey" was certainly necessary, but it was not easy to find the energy, space, and support to undertake it at a time when pastors needed to be profoundly present to others.

3. Palmer, *Insights on Leadership Service*, 15.

Part Four

Clergy Self-Care Protocol

THEMES THAT EMERGE FROM the survey and focus groups have helped determine how a self-care protocol for clergy might look. In particular I would highlight:

- The congregation needs to be involved in reimaging wellness and its practice.

- Self-care for clergy and congregation is a dynamic relationship.

- Both clergy and congregation need to have and to deploy self-care language.

- Clergy and congregation must be able to explore together how they might cope with broader issues such as racial tension and political turmoil—and pandemics.

- Both clergy and congregation should recognize that self-care is not selfishness.

- The reality of quiet quitting among the clergy is demonstrated in their investing the minimum amount of time, energy, and attention to their pastoral responsibilities: clergy remain in place but focus more acutely on retiring, changing jobs, or simply leaving their current position

- Clergy mentorship has a significant role to play in self-care.

- Clergy need to be able to express their vulnerability.

- Dealing with multiple forms of loss and grief can be overwhelming.

Clergy as Healers

Is there no balm in Gilead? Is there no physician there? Why then is there no healing for the wound of my people? (Jer 8:22)

I recognize that most clergy think of themselves in some way as healers, attending to the wounds of others.[1] But what of their own wounds? Suffering can lead to withdrawal, isolation, and stigma. Helplessness and a lack of personal agency, whether at work or in personal relationships, can set in. Despair, hopelessness, humiliation, and shame are signs of an individual in crisis.

The injuries that can fester when clergy and congregation do not practice care for the pastor cause a loss of self-respect and human dignity for the clergy themselves and can also harm the institutional church. Ultimately a self-care protocol must aim to maintain and restore the clergy, and with them their congregations, and to safeguard and heal the healer.

Clergy self-care is an effective solution to Jeremiah's question cited at the start of this section. Yet stress, which begins as anxiety, is the greatest enemy of self-care. We must act quickly to reduce stress by enhancing resiliency, especially in times of crisis. Resilience is strength that can be accessed in the mental, physical, and spiritual domains in the face of adversity. Resilience has been defined as consisting of five major capacities: (1) the ability to experience reward and motivation in a positive and optimistic way; (2) the ability to work and be productive despite fear; (3) the adaptation of social behaviors to promote altruism, social bonding, and teamwork; (4) the use of cognitive/thinking skills to see negative experiences in a more "positive" light; and (5) the development of

---

1. Cynthia O. Lindner, *Varieties of Gifts: Multiplicity and the Well-Lived Pastoral Life* (Lanham, MD: Rowman & Littlefield, 2016).

meaning and spiritual purpose in life.[2] Resiliency research consistently shows the importance of maintaining strong, positive social relationships.

The clergy self-care protocol proposed here provides a practice guide to help clergy develop that resiliency. Self-care must incorporated as a concrete system within congregational policies and practices.

I wish to stress the debt that my clergy self-care protocol owes to the *New Self-Care Protocol: Practice Guide for Healthcare Practitioners and Staff*, which reviews the principles and practices of self-care.[3] Both concepts and language have been drawn from this work, adapted in light of the study undertaken here to be applicable to clergy.

The contents of this clergy self-care protocol can be adapted to each congregational setting. Clergy and their congregation, working together, can move forward even in a time of crisis. To do so, they must be constantly aware of the self-damage that can result from compassion fatigue and vicarious suffering. This clergy self-care protocol can provide a basis for denominational, congregational, and pastoral conversations around clergy self-care.

Clergy Self-Care Protocol

The Definition of Self-Care

Self-care is a natural state of wellness and well-being. Clergy work to create a healing church environment that provides a healthy and nurturing environment for those working and worshiping in that environment. The healing environment provides a place of safety, security, and restoration. Self-care begins with the creation of a nurturing physical environment where the achievement of excellence is fostered. Self-care occurs when the physical and emotional

2. Richard F. Mollica et al., *New Self-Care Protocol: Practice Guide for Healthcare Practitioners and Staff*, Harvard/MGH Trauma Programs, 2020 (https://hprtselfcare.org).

3. Mollica et al., *New Self-Care Protocol*.

health of the clergy overrides competing concerns, for example, for the church's financial health. A healing environment contributes to healthy self-care, which in turn leads to excellent pastoral care. A healthy care system protects its clergy by never permitting physically and emotionally damaging clergy self-sacrifice, or, indeed, bullying and/or organizational abuse. Self-care is ultimately an integrated and holistic approach to the promotion of resiliency and wellness, with a premium placed on thinking freely and working imaginatively and creatively in a biblically informed environment. The capacity to be a healthy and affectionate pastor, in both pastoral relationships and contexts beyond pastoring, is maximized. Pastoral self-care maximizes the health and well-being of the pastor and then, in turn, of the church community of which they are both a part and a leader.

Clergy Contract and Covenant

The understanding and realization of clergy self-care should be expressed in the contract and covenants of all those employed by the church.

Priorities

Clergy self-care is not selfishness. The occupational life of clergy can have a damaging impact on those with whom they are close. The problems that play out mentally and physically for clergy can generate similar symptoms for their loved ones.

Space should be offered to clergy such that they can find acceptance of mental health concerns in themselves and their families. Clergy should know that they will not be stigmatized should they or members of their family require psychological/spiritual care.

Peer Support

Clergy peer support and/or clergy supervision can be integral to clergy self-care, whether in person or online. Such support must not drift into "therapy" for which the participants are not prepared or qualified. But trusted colleagues can provide peer support in a noncritical and nonjudgmental atmosphere. If support is found in a group, the leader should model nonjudgment and allow for differences and freedom of expression. Rules and procedures for such interactions must establish a safe and secure trusted space for empathic communication. Aggression, criticism, and bullying have no place in such peer support. While conflict may occur, proper resolution can lead to a stronger learning experience.

Empathy Heals

In essence, an effective healing relationship consists of "two persons, working in a community, in a shared empathic partnership, to create a new world view."[4] But empathy is a double-edged sword. Pastors are "spiritual overseers"—they are constantly concerned for the spiritual well-being of their flock, which includes their mental and physical pains. A healing journey based upon an empathic partner is a key ingredient in the relief of suffering. But as healers, clergy are perhaps particularly vulnerable to being burdened by the pain of others. The pain of those they tend must not be allowed to become their pain. Vicarious suffering can overwhelm clergy. It can also become compassion fatigue, which prevents clergy from living into their call.

Prayer, Mindfulness, and Meditation

Mindfulness is defined by the American Psychological Association as "awareness of one's internal states and surroundings," awareness

---

4. Mollica et al., *New Self-Care Protocol*, 11.

that is a vital part of self-care.[5] It is performed by the individual focusing their attention on their breathing, thoughts, feelings, and sensations as they occur. That attention is nonjudgmental. Building through practice, the meditation can come to embrace ethical value qualities, such as loving-kindness, compassion, self-compassion, and forgiveness. Mediation can, for example, accompany prayer as a tool for regulating empathy, with compassion meditation allowing greater immersion in the care of those who are suffering. Deep breathing exercises, easy to lead and practice, can be used in relation to a traumatic interaction. Structured Christian meditation, a form of prayer, enhances awareness of the power and revelations of God.

Personal Self-Care Practices

Personal self-care practices are scientifically well-established health promotion instruments for the prevention and treatment of medical illnesses and the promotion of wellness and well-being. These practices build upon resiliency, promoting increased self-efficacy and agency. Poor self-care can lead clergy not just to be unable to perform as pastors but also to lose meaningful relations with family and friends.

Personal practices, as the survey participants in the study noted, can include eating in community, time away from screens, and pursuing hobbies. In particular, as they also indirectly demonstrate, exercise has with good reason been identified as a "miracle" drug that can improve mood, heighten positive feelings, and reduce depression and stress, leading to an overall higher quality of life. Simply a twenty-minute walk each day may help.

Denominations and congregations should consider the value of investment in evidence-based personal self-care programs for their clergy. One such example is the Benson-Henry Institute for Mind Body Medicine at Massachusetts General Hospital's Stress

---

5. See https://www.apa.org/topics/mindfulness.

Management and Resilience Training (SMART) program.[6] It explores healthy behaviors, social support, social activities that create vitality and prosperity, cognitive skills to avoid negative thinking distortions, positive psychology, and problem-solving skills, as well as acceptance, spiritual connectedness, and compassion training. A related nonclinical version is the Positivity and Resilience Training (PART) program, which "teaches participants self-care techniques to promote health, happiness and generalized wellbeing." Its use of "creativity, humor and adaptive thinking" may make it particularly relevant for some clergy.[7]

Healthy Environment

Healing and beauty can go hand in hand. A sterile or disordered environment can influence personal numbness or chaotic thinking. A healthy environment is not just about the physical setting—although location is certainly a contributing factor—for it requires also healthy interpersonal relationships and access to healing forces. Nature is of prime significance, whether outdoors, brought indoors, or in pictures or imagination. Animals can make a rewarding contribution here.

The spaces occupied by the pastor should be ordered and peaceful, stimulating of the senses. Poor physical upkeep of church facilities can add to stress. Chaos is the opposite of the beauty that helps well-being thrive.

Evaluation

How do clergy, congregations, and denominations know if their self-care efforts and protocols are helping to improve their well-being?

Clergy, congregations, and denominations must not just *establish* realistic self-care goals but also invest in exploring whether

---

6. https://bensonhenryinstitute.org/smart-program/.

7. https://bensonhenryinstitute.org/training-part-training/.

they have been *realized*. Simple quantitative methods and surveys can determine which self-care practices have been implemented, frequency of practice and attendance, and staff motivation and interest in using these practices. Outcomes can include a healthier lifestyle, greater family engagement, and the prevention/reduction of the symptoms of burnout, compassion fatigue, and secondary traumatization. While many validated scales exist to assess outcomes, each congregation's self-care protocol will be focused on more than the prevention of illness or unhealthy or dysfunctional churches. Each congregation should therefore consider carefully what effective self-care will look like in its own context.

Epilogue

Trauma-Informed Ministry

IN 2014 I EXPLORED and wrote about "trauma-informed ministry." With COVID-19, those lessons seemed to gain a new relevance. Even a pastor who sought and practiced self-care was now serving a congregation in great pain, a congregation that might be defined as "traumatized." Trauma, the Council on Social Work Education has observed,

> results from adverse life experiences that overwhelm an individual's capacity to cope and to adapt positively to whatever threat he or she faces. . . . Trauma exposure's lasting impact represents a combination of the event and the subjective thoughts and feelings it engenders. An event becomes traumatic when its adverse effect produces feelings of helplessness and lack of control, and thoughts that one's survival may possibly be in danger.[1]

In a text on self-care, we can usefully also look outwards, too, into the world that the pastor is serving:

A trauma-informed ministry is one by which religious care providers have a basic understanding of the nature of trauma and how it may impact the overall quality of life of the person or

---

1. Quoted in Frederick Streets, "Frederick Streets: The Urgent Need for Trauma Informed Ministry," *Middletown Press*, June 5, 2014, para. 1 (https://www.middletownpress.com/opinion/article/Frederick-Streets-The-urgent-need-for-trauma-11795179.php).

persons who have been traumatized by a life event and the impact of that trauma on their relationships with other people.

A trauma-informed ministry seeks to sensitively use a basic understanding of trauma and reflect upon its implications for the various aspects of a religious ministry such as preaching, Bible study, prayer, and other religious rituals and spiritual practices.

A trauma-informed ministry means that the religious care provider is aware of the impact of trauma upon persons depending upon where they are along the life cycle, as well as their age, gender, social and marital status, and sexual orientation.

A trauma-informed ministry brings to bear upon those suffering from trauma the wisdom, insights, and resources of the religious faith and tradition of those who have been traumatized and utilizes these cultural attributes for the sufferer's benefit.

A trauma-informed ministry seeks to collaborate with other community members who can provide additional resources and to whom the religious helper can refer those needing assistance in coping with their traumatic experiences.

A trauma-informed ministry aims to increase the skills of coping with or reducing the stress that can otherwise lead the sufferer to feel that they can no longer manage or prevent their traumatic and post-traumatic experience from destroying them. It is important to remember that a trauma-informed ministry understands the vulnerability of people and the tenuous nature of their sense of safety. Most importantly, those who have been traumatized need to be encouraged and supported in being hopeful about their own recovery. One of the most significant impacts of suffering from trauma is the stigma associated with needing help to deal with the traumatic experience. The shame that some people feel because of having been traumatized prevents them from seeking help.

Religious helpers can play a vital role in reducing such shame by reminding those suffering from trauma that getting help is a sign of their strength. But clergy should also remember that there is no shame in their reaching out for help themselves—a core principle of effective pastoral self-care.

Appendix 1

For this study, participants completed three surveys on-line: "Clergy Demographics," "Clergy Well-Being," and "Clergy Self-Care."

All three surveys were available through a single portal.[1]

They are included here as a result of their relevance to the discussion in this book, but also in order that they might spur conversation as clergy, denominations, and congregations discuss their own self-care protocols for clergy.

Survey One: Clergy Demographics

Q1.1   Current age _____

Q1.2   Gender self-identification

- Male
- Female
- Other

---

1. https://jerrystreets.org/clergy-well-being-surveys/.

Q1.3   What is your self-identified ethnic group?

- African American/Black
- Hispanic American/Latino/Spanish origin
- Asian American
- Native American/Alaskan Native
- Caucasian American
- Middle Eastern or North African
- Native Hawaiian or other Pacific Islander
- Other

Q1.4   How long have you served as an ordained religious professional? _____

Q1.5   Please select all that apply to your current primary context of serving as clergy, and enter the number of years in each that you select.

- Parish/congregational minister
- Institutional/chaplain
- Denominational officer/executive leader
- Rural
- Urban
- Suburban
- Average number of attendees on Sunday
- Virtual
- In-person

Q1.6   Number of months church was online during the pandemic _____

Q1.7   Do you work in any of the educational institutional set-
        tings below? Click to select all that apply and indicate
        number of years for each one you select.

- Primary school _____
- High school _____
- College _____
- Graduate/professional school _____

Q1.8   Please briefly describe below your primary context of
        serving as clergy. _____

Q1.9   Are you full-time or part-time in your current primary
        context of work as clergy?

- Full-time
- Part-time

Q1.10   Number of paid authorized ministers on staff _____

Q1.11   Number of paid staff _____

Q1.12   Number of volunteers available in congregation _____

Q1.13   Number of tech staff _____

Q1.14   Please briefly describe if you currently have any primary
        care giving responsibilities (children/elders). _____

Q1.15   Have you had or are you currently having any conflicts
        within the church or work setting around COVID proto-
        cols? Please describe. _____

Q1.16   Please briefly describe the financial impact the pandemic
        has on you personally and professionally._____

Q1.17   Briefly describe your support system since the beginning
        of the pandemic._____

Q1.18   Please describe your general physical and mental health
        status before and since the pandemic. _____

Q1.19   Please feel free to add below anything you would further like to share. _____

Survey Two: Clergy Well-Being

During the past month . . .

Q2.1   Have you felt burned out from your work?

- No
- Yes

Q2.2   Have you worried that your work is hardening you emotionally?

- No
- Yes

Q2.3   Have you often been bothered by feeling down, depressed, or hopeless?

- No
- Yes

Q2.4   Have you fallen asleep while sitting inactive in a public place?

- No
- Yes

Q2.5   Have you felt that all the things you had to do were piling up so high that you could not overcome them?

- No
- Yes

Q2.6 Have you been bothered by emotional problems (such as feeling anxious, depressed, or irritable)?

- No
- Yes

Q2.7 Has your physical health interfered with your ability to do your daily work at home and/or away from home?

- No
- Yes

Q2.8 The work I do is meaningful to me:

- Strongly disagree
- Disagree
- Somewhat disagree
- Neither agree nor disagree
- Somewhat agree
- Agree

Q2.9 My work schedule leaves me enough time for my personal/family life

- Strongly disagree
- Disagree
- Somewhat disagree
- Neither agree nor disagree
- Somewhat agree
- Agree

Survey Three: Clergy Self-Care

For each question check the option that reflects the frequency of your behavior (how much or how often) within the past week (7 days).

Mindful Relaxation

Q3.1   I did something intellectual (using my mind) to help me relax (e.g., read a book, wrote).

- Never (0 days)
- Rarely (1 day)
- Sometimes (2 to 3 days)
- Often (4 to 5 days)
- Regularly (6 to 7 days)

Q3.2   I did something interpersonal to relax (e.g., connected with friends).

- Never (0 days)
- Rarely (1 day)
- Sometimes (2 to 3 days)
- Often (4 to 5 days)
- Regularly (6 to 7 days)

Q3.3   I did something creative to relax (e.g., drew, played instrument, wrote creatively, sang).

- Never (0 days)
- Rarely (1 day)
- Sometimes (2 to 3 days)
- Often (4 to 5 days)
- Regularly (6 to 7 days)

Q3.4   I listened to relax (e.g., to music, a podcast, radio show, rainforest sounds).

- Never (0 days)
- Rarely (1 day)
- Sometimes (2 to 3 days)
- Often (4 to 5 days)
- Regularly (6 to 7 days)

Q3.5   I sought out images to relax (e.g., art, film, window shopping, nature).

- Never (0 days)
- Rarely (1 day)
- Sometimes (2 to 3 days)
- Often (4 to 5 days)
- Regularly (6 to 7 days)

Q3.6   I sought out smells to relax (lotions, nature, candles/incense, baking).

- Never (0 days)
- Rarely (1 day)
- Sometimes (2 to 3 days)
- Often (4 to 5 days)
- Regularly (6 to 7 days)

Physical Care

Q3.7   I drank at least six to eight cups of water.

- Never (o days)
- Rarely (1 day)
- Sometimes (2 to 3 days)
- Often (4 to 5 days)
- Regularly (6 to 7 days)

Q3.8   I ate a variety of nutritious foods (e.g., vegetables, protein, fruits, and grains).

- Never (o days)
- Rarely (1 day)
- Sometimes (2 to 3 days)
- Often (4 to 5 days)
- Regularly (6 to 7 days)

Q3.9   I planned my meals and snacks.

- Never (o days)
- Rarely (1 day)
- Sometimes (2 to 3 days)
- Often (4 to 5 days)
- Regularly (6 to 7 days)

Q3.10   I exercised at least thirty to sixty minutes.

- Never (o days)
- Rarely (1 day)
- Sometimes (2 to 3 days)
- Often (4 to 5 days)
- Regularly (6 to 7 days)

Q3.11   I took part in sports, dance, or other scheduled physical
         activities (e.g., sports teams, dance classes).

- Never (0 days)
- Rarely (1 day)
- Sometimes (2 to 3 days)
- Often (4 to 5 days)
- Regularly (6 to 7 days)

Q3.12   I did sedentary activities (e.g., watched TV, worked on the
         computer).

- Never (0 days)
- Rarely (1 day)
- Sometimes (2 to 3 days)
- Often (4 to 5 days)
- Regularly (6 to 7 days)

Q3.13   I planned/scheduled my exercise for the day.

- Never (0 days)
- Rarely (1 day)
- Sometimes (2 to 3 days)
- Often (4 to 5 days)
- Regularly (6 to 7 days)

Q3.14   I practiced yoga or another mind/body practice (e.g., tae
         kwon do, tai chi).

- Never (0 days)
- Rarely (1 day)
- Sometimes (2 to 3 days)
- Often (4 to 5 days)
- Regularly (6 to 7 days)

Self-Compassion and Purpose

Q3.15   I kindly acknowledged my own challenges and difficulties.

- Never (0 days)
- Rarely (1 day)
- Sometimes (2 to 3 days)
- Often (4 to 5 days)
- Regularly (6 to 7 days)

Q3.16   I engaged in supportive and comforting self-talk (e.g., "My effort is valuable and meaningful").

- Never (0 days)
- Rarely (1 day)
- Sometimes (2 to 3 days)
- Often (4 to 5 days)
- Regularly (6 to 7 days)

Q3.17   I reminded myself that failure and challenge are part of the human experience.

- Never (0 days)
- Rarely (1 day)
- Sometimes (2 to 3 days)
- Often (4 to 5 days)
- Regularly (6 to 7 days)

Q3.18   I gave myself permission to feel my feelings (e.g., allowed myself to cry).

- Never (0 days)
- Rarely (1 day)
- Sometimes (2 to 3 days)
- Often (4 to 5 days)
- Regularly (6 to 7 days)

Q3.19   I experienced meaning and/or a larger purpose in my work life (e.g., for a cause).

- Never (0 days)
- Rarely (1 day)
- Sometimes (2 to 3 days)
- Often (4 to 5 days)
- Regularly (6 to 7 days)

Q3.20   I experienced meaning and/or a larger purpose in my private/personal life (e.g., for a cause).

- Never (0 days)
- Rarely (1 day)
- Sometimes (2 to 3 days)
- Often (4 to 5 days)
- Regularly (6 to 7 days)

Supportive Relationships

Q3.21   I spent time with people who are good to me (e.g., support, encourage, and believe in me).

- Never (0 days)
- Rarely (1 day)
- Sometimes (2 to 3 days)
- Often (4 to 5 days)
- Regularly (6 to 7 days)

Q3.22   I scheduled/planned time to be with people who are special to me.

- Never (0 days)
- Rarely (1 day)
- Sometimes (2 to 3 days)
- Often (4 to 5 days)
- Regularly (6 to 7 days)

Q3.23   I felt supported by people in my life.

- Never (0 days)
- Rarely (1 day)
- Sometimes (2 to 3 days)
- Often (4 to 5 days)
- Regularly (6 to 7 days)

Q3.24   I felt confident that people in my life would respect my choice if I said no.

- Never (0 days)
- Rarely (1 day)
- Sometimes (2 to 3 days)
- Often (4 to 5 days)
- Regularly (6 to 7 days)

Q3.25   I felt that I had someone who would listen to me if I became upset (e.g., friend, counselor, group).

- Never (0 days)
- Rarely (1 day)
- Sometimes (2 to 3 days)
- Often (4 to 5 days)
- Regularly (6 to 7 days)

Supportive Structure

Q3.26   I maintained a manageable schedule.

- Never (0 days)
- Rarely (1 day)
- Sometimes (2 to 3 days)
- Often (4 to 5 days)
- Regularly (6 to 7 days)

Q3.27   I kept my work area organized to support my work tasks.

- Never (0 days)
- Rarely (1 day)
- Sometimes (2 to 3 days)
- Often (4 to 5 days)
- Regularly (6 to 7 days)

Q3.28   I maintained balance between the demands of others and what is important to me.

- Never (0 days)
- Rarely (1 day)
- Sometimes (2 to 3 days)
- Often (4 to 5 days)
- Regularly (6 to 7 days)

Q3.29   I maintained a comforting and pleasing living environment.

- Never (0 days)
- Rarely (1 day)
- Sometimes (2 to 3 days)
- Often (4 to 5 days)
- Regularly (6 to 7 days)

Mindful Awareness

Q3.30 I had a calm awareness of my thoughts.

- Never (0 days)
- Rarely (1 day)
- Sometimes (2 to 3 days)
- Often (4 to 5 days)
- Regularly (6 to 7 days)

Q3.31 I had a calm awareness of my feelings.

- Never (0 days)
- Rarely (1 day)
- Sometimes (2 to 3 days)
- Often (4 to 5 days)
- Regularly (6 to 7 days)

Q3.32 I had a calm awareness of my body.

- Never (0 days)
- Rarely (1 day)
- Sometimes (2 to 3 days)
- Often (4 to 5 days)
- Regularly (6 to 7 days)

Q3.33 I carefully selected which of my thoughts and feelings I used to guide my actions.

- Never (0 days)
- Rarely (1 day)
- Sometimes (2 to 3 days)
- Often (4 to 5 days)
- Regularly (6 to 7 days)

APPENDIX 1

Overview

Q3.34   I engaged in a variety of self-care activities.

- Never (0 days)
- Rarely (1 day)
- Sometimes (2 to 3 days)
- Often (4 to 5 days)
- Regularly (6 to 7 days)

Q3.35   I planned my self-care.

- Never (0 days)
- Rarely (1 day)
- Sometimes (2 to 3 days)
- Often (4 to 5 days)
- Regularly (6 to 7 days)

Q3.36   I explored new ways to bring self-care into my life.

- Never (0 days)
- Rarely (1 day)
- Sometimes (2 to 3 days)
- Often (4 to 5 days)
- Regularly (6 to 7 days)

Appendix 2

Hypotheses and Their Testing

Hypothesis 1: Total MSCS scores would be negatively correlated with PWBI scores. SCP who engaged in mindful self-care practices would experience higher well-being, as operationalized by lowered PWBI scores.

Hypothesis 2: Mindful self-care practices would be negatively correlated with PWBI scores. Some mindful self-care practices will be stronger protective factors against lowered well-being, as operationalized by the PWBI.

Hypothesis 3: Demographic variables will not be statistically significant predictors of well-being among SCPs.

Hypothesis 4: Clergy will have significantly higher mindful self-care scores than published MSCS norms data.

The PWBI, MSCS total, and subscales were scored using the prescribed coding methods in their manuals. A missing value analysis was performed in SPSS v24. Listwise deletion was utilized in these cases.

Pearson correlation tests were performed to describe the correlations between each of the following: the PWBI, MSCS total, and each of the MSCS subscales. A multiple regression model was used to test predictors of PWBI while controlling for the demographic variables of age, gender, ethnicity, and employment status on PWBI.

Table 1 shows correlations, means, and standard deviations of all study variables.

There was a moderate, negative association between overall MSCS and PWBI ($r = -.505, p < .01$). In addition, table 1 illustrates that MSCS predicted PWBI (ß = .255, $p < .01$). Stated another way, the effect size of MSCS on PWBI was 25.5 percent. Thus, the null hypothesis of hypothesis 1 was rejected. Overall MSCS was negatively correlated with PWBI scores with statistical significance. SCP who engaged in mindful self-care experienced higher well-being, as operationalized by lowered PWBI scores. This was expected and fits with prior findings from other studies.

The null hypothesis of hypothesis 2 was also rejected. Frequent and varied self-care practices were protective factors against lowered well-being. All mindful self-care practices were negatively correlated with PWBI scores. Two mindful self-care practices were stronger protective factors against lowered well-being: supportive structure ($r = -.604, p < .01$) and supportive relationships ($r = -.466, p < .01$) were the strongest protective factors. The remaining practices varied between $-.230$ to $-.414$, each with statistical significance ($p < .01$).

The null hypothesis of hypothesis 3 was rejected. Demographic variables were not statistically significant predictors of well-being among clergy. Table 1 displays model 1, the demographics model, which included the participants' variables: age, gender, ethnicity, and employment status. Only age was a statistically significant predictor of PWBI (ß = $-.255, p < .01$).

Finally, the null hypothesis of hypothesis 4 was rejected for all self-care factors. For each of the mindful self-care subscales and the MSCS combined, the clergy in this study had higher self-care scores (frequency of practice) than published norms. Table 1 reports Mnorm and tnorm for all self-care factors, mean scores, and the MSCS mean; tnorm ranged from 4.08 to 9.39, $p < .001$. This result means that the clergy in this study had more frequent self-care practices than the general population.

Appendix 2

Variable	M	SD	M_{norm}	t_{norm}	1	2	3	4	5	6	7	8	9	10
1. Mindful Relaxation (MR)	3.17	.77	2.99	4.08**	1									
2. Physical Care (PC)	3.05	.75	2.87	4.32**	.505**	1								
3. Self-Compassion and Purpose (SC)	3.67	.74	3.33	8.32**	.545**	.405**	1							
4. Supportive Relationships (SR)	4.01	.76	3.75	5.99**	.449**	.370**	.581**	1						
5. Supportive Structure (SS)	3.76	.78	3.40	8.20**	.335**	.333**	.352**	.519**	1					
6. Mindful Awareness (MA)	3.77	.81	3.35	9.38**	.535**	.446**	.636**	.469**	.441**	1				
7. Mindful Self-Care (MSCS)	21.43	3.43	19.69	9.06**	.769**	.746**	.773**	.726**	.610**	.745**	1			
8. General MSCS Questions	3.21	.93	–	–	.606**	.629**	.602**	.528**	.469**	.607**	.775**	1		
9. Physician Well-Being Index (PWBI)	2.67	1.92	–	–	-.352**	-.329**	-.230**	-.466**	-.604**	-.414**	-.505**	-.400**	1	
10. Age range (25–87 years)	59.5	12.1	–	–	.250**	.198**	.171**	.141**	.229**	.234**	.200**	.251**	-.241**	1

Notes. ** p < .01, * p < .05

93

Made in the USA
Middletown, DE
12 September 2024

60867550R00066